THE NBA LIBRARY

ABOVE THE RIM

PACIFIC DIVISION

BY TED BROCK

THE GOLDEN STATE WARRIORS
THE LOS ANGELES CLIPPERS
THE LOS ANGELES LAKERS
THE PHOENIX SUNS
THE PORTLAND TRAIL BLAZERS
THE SACRAMENTO KINGS
THE SEATTLE SUPERSONICS

Note to readers:

At press time, the NBA was considering a plan that would reorganize the league into six divisions of five teams, beginning in the 2004-05 season. It will also add a 30th team, the Charlotte Bobcats.

THE PACIFIC DIVISION: The Golden State Warriors, the Los Angeles Clippers, the Los Angeles Lakers, the Phoenix Suns, the Portland Trail Blazers, the Sacramento Kings, and the Seattle SuperSonics

Published in the United States of America by The Child's World®
PO Box 326 • Chanhassen, MN 55317-0326 • 800-599-READ • www.childsworld.com

ACKNOWLEDGEMENTS:
The Child's World®: Mary Berendes, Publishing Director

Editorial Directions, Inc.: E. Russell Primm, Editorial Director and Line Editor; Katie Marsico, Assistant Editor; Matthew Messbarger, Editorial Assistant; Susan Hindman, Copy Editor; Melissa McDaniel, Proofreader; Tim Griffin, Indexer; Kevin Cunningham, Fact Checker; James Buckley Jr., Photo Reseacher and Photo Selector

The Design Lab: Kathleen Petelinsek, Designer and Production Artist

PHOTOS:
Cover: AFP/Corbis
AP/Wide World: 10, 25, 38, 40.
Bettman/Corbis: 5, 7, 8, 13, 15, 16, 18, 26, 28, 30, 33, 35, 36, 44.
Sports Gallery: 9, 14, 19, 20, 29.

LIBRARY OF CONGRESS CATALOGING-IN-PUBLICATION DATA
Brock, Ted.
The Pacific Division: the Golden State Warriors, the Los Angeles Clippers, the Los Angeles Lakers, the Phoenix Suns, the Portland Trail Blazers, the Sacramento Kings, and the Seattle Supersonics / by Ted Brock.
    p. cm. — (Above the rim)
Summary: Describes the seven teams that make up the Pacific Division of the National Basketball Association, their histories, famous players, and statistics.
Includes bibliographical references and index.
  ISBN 1-59296-206-8 (lib. bdg. : alk. paper)
1. National Basketball Association—History—Juvenile literature. 2. Basketball—West (U.S.)—History—Juvenile literature. [1. National Basketball Association—History. 2. Basketball.] I. Title. II. Series.
GV885.515.N37B76 2004
796.323'64'0973—dc22

                        2003020034

The National Basketball Association's (NBA) Pacific Division officially began play in 1970. But three of its seven franchises—Oakland's Golden State Warriors, the Los Angeles Lakers, and the Sacramento Kings—date back to the earliest days of the NBA, which was formed in 1946. In the first 57 years of the league, four of the division's franchises won a combined total of 19 NBA championships.

By adding Pacific Division members Seattle, Portland, Phoenix, and Sacramento to the NBA's geography, the league made itself truly national. Each new city has taken the game to its heart. Pacific Division teams have included NBA legends such as George Mikan, Elgin Baylor, Oscar Robertson, Jerry West, Rick Barry, and Wilt Chamberlain. More recent stars include Nate "Tiny" Archibald, Bill Walton, Kareem Abdul-Jabbar, Earvin "Magic" Johnson, James Worthy, Shaquille O'Neal, and Kobe Bryant.

For competition and entertainment, the Pacific Division holds its own with any in the NBA. Just ask the 2002–03 Lakers. Trying for a fourth straight championship, they got a fight from division rivals Sacramento, Portland, and Phoenix. Meanwhile, the Seattle SuperSonics and the Golden State Warriors showed signs of coming back. That left only the seventh-place Los Angeles Clippers dreaming of becoming a regular contender.

The NBA first reached the Pacific Coast in 1960, when the Lakers moved west from Minneapolis. In 1985, the Pacific Division's seventh and final team, the Kings, completed its long journey to Sacramento from Rochester, New York. Along the way, this team that was once known as the Royals made stops in Cincinnati, Kansas City, and Omaha. It's only fitting that the Kings, winners of the Pacific Division in 2002–03, have left such a deep imprint on the NBA map.

Mike Bibby and Sacramento had lots to cheer about in 2003.

TEAM	YEAR FOUNDED	HOME ARENA	YEAR ARENA OPENED	TEAM COLORS
GOLDEN STATE WARRIORS	1946	THE ARENA IN OAKLAND	1997	DARK BLUE & GOLD
LOS ANGELES CLIPPERS	1970	STAPLES CENTER	1999	RED, WHITE, & BLUE
LOS ANGELES LAKERS	1946	STAPLES CENTER	1999	PURPLE & GOLD
PHOENIX SUNS	1968	AMERICA WEST ARENA	1992	RED, ORANGE, & WHITE
PORTLAND TRAIL BLAZERS	1970	ROSE GARDEN	1995	RED, BLACK, & WHITE
SACRAMENTO KINGS	1948	ARCO ARENA	1988	PURPLE, SILVER, & BLACK
SEATTLE SUPERSONICS	1967	KEYARENA	1995	GREEN & GOLD

CHAPTER 1

THE GOLDEN STATE WARRIORS

I t's hard to find an NBA franchise whose history contains more colorful characters than the Golden State Warriors. The club was one of the original 11 franchises in the Basketball Association of America, one of the fore-runners of the NBA. The Warriors, led by league-leading scorer "Jumpin' Joe" Fulks, were champions in the NBA's first season, 1946–47.

Eddie Gottlieb was the team's original owner, general manager, and coach. Gottlieb remained owner until 1962 but named former Warriors guard George Senesky coach in 1955. Senesky led the team to the 1955–56 NBA title, defeating the Fort Wayne Pistons in five games, thanks in large part to rookie guard Tom Gola.

Seven-foot-two Wilt "Stilt" Chamberlain, considered by many the greatest **center** in NBA history, joined the Warriors in 1959. Among his many scoring records, Chamberlain—whose epic battles with Boston center Bill Russell will always hold a special

There never had been a scorer like Wilt Chamberlain before . . . or since.

place in NBA history—set the league's single-game scoring record with a 100-point performance in a 1962 game.

Chamberlain led the NBA in scoring in all six of his seasons with the Warriors and in rebounding five times during that stretch. His 50.4 points per game in 1961–62 is a league record.

In 1962, the Warriors moved to San Francisco. Their first season under new owner Franklin Mieuli saw them sink to a 31–49 record, fourth in the NBA's Western Division. (Mieuli was quite a character. He sometimes drove his motorcycle to work—right down the hallway and into his office!) But in 1963–64, guided by new head coach Alex Hannum, the team finished 48–32 in the **regular season** and

Rick Barry was a deft shooter and a brilliant passer.

made it to the **NBA Finals.** They lost there in five games to Boston, giving the Celtics their sixth straight title.

The Warriors won only 17 games and sank to last place in the West in 1964–65, the year they traded Chamberlain to the Philadelphia 76ers. In 1965–66, they picked up Rick Barry—like Chamberlain and Nate Thurmond, a future Hall of Famer. But in 1967, Barry jumped to the Oakland Oaks of the new American Basketball Association.

The Warriors moved to Oakland to begin the 1971–72 season and became known as Golden State. Barry returned to the team for the 1972–73 season, and in 1974, the club traded Thurmond to Chicago for center Clifford Ray. Barry, Ray, and

Center Nate Thurmond was a big-time
player on offense and defense.

veteran guard Jeff Mullins played key roles for head coach and former Warriors guard Al Attles. The Warriors won the 1974–75 NBA championship, sweeping the Washington Bullets in four games.

It was the last taste of success the team would know. The Warriors' fortunes rose briefly in the late 1970s, then sank in the early and mid-1980s. In 1986, Mieuli sold the team to Jim Fitzgerald and Dan Finnane, who hired new head coach George Karl. The Warriors, led by center Joe Barry Carroll and **point guard** Eric "Sleepy" Floyd, made the

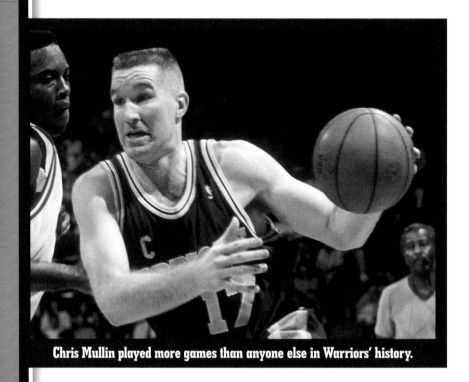

Chris Mullin played more games than anyone else in Warriors' history.

1986–87 **playoffs** and reached the Western Conference semifinals.

In the early 1990s, coach Don Nelson's "Run TMC" teams featured flashy guard Tim Hardaway, sharpshooting forward Chris Mullin, and talented center Chris Webber. "Run TMC" (named using the initials of Tim, Mullin and Chris) helped the Warriors reach the playoffs in 1993–94. In 1994–95, the Warriors peaked with a 50–32 regular-season finish.

In 1995–96, the team got a lift, winning 36 games after the arrival of forward Joe Smith and with the help of guard Latrell Sprewell. But in 1998, Sprewell was traded to New York after assaulting coach P. J. Carlesimo during practice.

Over the next few years, five coaches took turns leading the team as it spun downward to its worst record ever (17–65) in 2000–01.

In 2002–03, Golden State won more than 30 games for the first time since 1995–96 and wasn't out of playoff contention until the last two weeks. Youngsters such as sharpshooting Jason Richardson and forward Troy Murphy give the club bright hopes for the future.

Former Warriors star Rick Barry is the only player ever to lead the NCAA, NBA, and ABA in scoring. He was a deadly accurate free-throw shooter who made a remarkable 90 per-cent of his career attempts from the line—by shooting the ball underhand!

THE LOS ANGELES CLIPPERS

The Clippers—there's no other way to put this—are the Pacific Division's weakest team. It's been that way most of the franchise's history. In its first 33 seasons, the franchise record was 952 victories and 1,722 losses. They won just 36 percent of their games.

The team was born in 1970 as the Buffalo Braves, owned by John Y. Brown and coached by Hall of Fame player Dolph Schayes, who was fired the following season after only one game. For the first two seasons, the Braves had identical 22–60 records. But they began a three-year playoff run in 1974 under head coach Jack Ramsay and with the leadership of future Hall of Famer Bob McAdoo. Ramsay left in 1976 to coach the Portland Trail Blazers, and the Braves had four head coaches in the next two seasons.

The team changed its nickname to Clippers when it moved from New York to the port city of San Diego, California, in 1978. Its new owner was

California businessman Irv Levin, who had been the Boston Celtics' owner but traded teams with Brown prior to the move. In 1981, Levin sold the team to real estate developer Donald T. Sterling, who moved the Clippers to Los Angeles in 1984.

During its first 14 years in California, the team did not make the playoffs under head coaches Cotton Fitzsimmons, Gene Shue, Paul Silas, Jim Lynam, Don Chaney, Don Casey, and Mike Schuler. Among its top players during that period were forwards Tom Chambers, Terry Cummings, and Michael Cage.

High-scoring Bob McAdoo helped make the Braves a playoff team.

Well-traveled coach Larry Brown stopped in L.A. from 1992-93.

The 1991–92 team began the season under Schuler, had Mack Calvin as head coach for two games, and then hired coach Larry Brown, who was 23–12 in his last 35 games. Led by forward Danny Manning and guards Ron Harper and Glenn "Doc" Rivers, the team made the playoffs. The following season, they again made the playoffs for the second straight year, but lost in the first round. Guard Mark Jackson joined the Clippers before the 1993–94 season.

After one year under head coach Bob Weiss, the Clippers hired Bill Fitch, who lasted four years. His third season, 1996–97, produced what would be the Clippers' most recent playoff appearance, featuring the leadership of forward Loy Vaught, the team's high scorer and rebounder.

The Clippers hope Corey Maggette can help
take them to new heights.

Young star Elton Brand led the Clippers in scoring in 2002-03.

The franchise record for points in a game is 52. Charles Smith was the last Clippers' player to reach that figure, doing so in a 137-121 victory over Denver on December 1, 1990.

The Clippers, always a team of high hopes, followed the Fitch era with one and a half seasons under Chris Ford, half a season under Jim Todd, and two and a half seasons under Alvin Gentry, before hiring former Seattle and Boston star Dennis Johnson midway through the 2002–03 season. Johnson has since been replaced veteran NBA coach Mike Dunleavy.

In 1999–2000, the team moved from the Los Angeles Sports Arena just up the street to Staples Center, where it drew much larger crowds. Forward Elton Brand and swingman Corey Maggette had become the heart of the team and the main hope for bringing the Clippers to life.

CHAPTER 3

THE LOS ANGELES LAKERS

Lakers' history is rich with championships and superstars, and the team's 14 NBA championships are second only to the Boston Celtics' 16. The Lakers joined the NBA as an original member, and they have managed to stay at or near the top of the pro basketball world.

The Minneapolis Lakers, coached by John Kundla, became pro basketball's first true **dynasty** under the leadership of center George Mikan. They won the championship four out of five times between the 1948–49 and 1952–53 seasons, missing only the 1950–51 title. Mikan was pro basketball's first media star and its dominant big man, playing for a team nicknamed after its state's well-known "10,000 Lakes" slogan. The club kept its nickname when owner Bob Short moved the franchise to Los Angeles before the 1960–61 season.

The Lakers already had picked up Seattle University All-America forward Elgin Baylor in the

If Jerry West's form looks familiar, it's because it's the NBA logo.

1958 **draft,** and in 1960 they grabbed another future Hall of Famer, West Virginia guard Jerry West. With West came his college coach, Fred Schaus, and the team began making regular appearances in the NBA Finals.

Short sold the team to Jack Kent Cooke in 1965. In 1968, Cooke obtained star center Wilt Chamberlain in a trade with the Philadelphia 76ers. Still for the fifth time since 1959, the Lakers lost to the Celtics in the NBA Finals. Joe Mullaney replaced Bill van Breda Kolff (who replaced Schaus

Kareem Abdul-Jabbar is the NBA's all-time leading scorer.

Jerry West made one of the most famous shots in NBA history, sinking a 60-foot heave at the buzzer to force overtime against the Knicks in Game 3 of the 1970 Finals. But New York went on to win the game and the series.

before the 1967–68 season) as head coach in 1969, and in 1970 Mullaney took the team to yet another NBA Finals appearance. The Lakers lost to the New York Knicks—the seventh time in nine years they'd been to the finals and left empty-handed.

The 1971–72 Lakers, coached by former Celtics guard Bill Sharman, won 33 games in a row—still a professional sports record. Baylor retired at the beginning of the season, but the lineup of Chamberlain, West, guard Gail Goodrich, and

His real name is Earvin Johnson, but the world knows him as Magic.

forwards Jim McMillian and Happy Hairston won 69 games in the regular season and defeated the Knicks four games to one for the NBA title.

The Lakers picked up the league's best big man, Kareem Abdul-Jabbar, in 1975. It wasn't until 1979, with the arrival of 6-foot-9 guard Earvin "Magic" Johnson, that "Showtime" became the Lakers' style and slogan.

New owner Jerry Buss, who bought the Lakers from Cooke in 1979, had a winner in his first season. They defeated Philadelphia in six games for the NBA championship. Abdul-Jabbar was named the league's Most Valuable Player for the sixth and final time.

The Lakers were knocked out of the playoffs the following year. The club fired head coach Paul Westhead during the 1981–82 season and hired Pat Riley for what would be a successful nine-year run. The team won 17 of its first 20 games under Riley and went on to defeat Philadelphia in the NBA Finals, 4–2.

The Lakers added future Hall of Famer James Worthy in 1982–83, and in 1983–84, the year Abdul-Jabbar became the NBA's all-time scoring

Magic Johnson was just a 20-year-old rookie when he moved from guard to center to replace injured Kareem Abdul-Jabbar in Game 6 of the 1980 NBA Finals. Johnson scored 42 points and grabbed 15 rebounds to lead the Lakers to a title-clinching win.

leader with 31,420 points, they reached the finals, where they lost to the Celtics in seven games.

They broke Boston's spell in 1984–85, beating the Celtics in the finals for the first time in nine championship match-ups. The Lakers beat the Celtics again in the 1986–87 finals and repeated as champions by beating the Detroit Pistons in seven games to win the title in 1987–88.

In 1988–89, Abdul-Jabbar retired at age 41 after 20 seasons in the NBA. Riley retired in 1990 after nine years as head coach. In November 1991, Magic Johnson announced his retirement, revealing that he had HIV, the virus that causes AIDS. Magic would make two separate comebacks, in 1993–94 and 1995–96.

After Riley, the Lakers tried a series of six coaches—Mike Dunleavy, Randy Pfund, Magic Johnson, Del Harris, Bill Bertka, and Kurt Rambis—until the arrival of Phil Jackson in 1999. The 1996–97 season brought the Lakers massive center Shaquille O'Neal and an 18-year-old rookie named Kobe Bryant. In 1999–2000, Shaq and Kobe led the Lakers to the first of three consecu-tive NBA championships.

THE PHOENIX SUNS

You can trace the 35-year journey of the Phoenix franchise through the careers of six players: Dick Van Arsdale, Paul Westphal, Alvan Adams, Walter Davis, Kevin Johnson, and Tom Chambers.

Phoenix joined the NBA as an expansion franchise in 1968, and after a name-the-team contest drew 28,000 entries, the club chose the one that was there in broad daylight all the time. The newly christened Suns chose Van Arsdale in the expansion draft, and he ended up making three All-Star teams in his nine seasons with the team.

The Suns made their first playoff appearance in 1969–70. In 1975, they picked up Westphal from Boston, and in 1975–76, they reached the finals before falling to the Celtics. The player who led Phoenix's rise was Adams, a 6-foot-9 center from Oklahoma who earned Rookie of the Year honors. He spent his full 13-year career with the Suns.

Davis, a 6-foot-6 **small forward** with a sweet

shooting touch, played 11 seasons with the Suns
(1977–88). During the 1987–88 season, the Suns
got point guard Johnson in a trade with Cleveland.
"KJ," a three-time NBA All-Star and a member of
Dream Team 2 at the World Championships of
Basketball in 1994, would come out of retirement
in 2000 to fortify the Suns in the playoff drive
when star point guard Jason Kidd broke his ankle.

The team's early rise in the Pacific Division
came under head coach John MacLeod. He took
the Suns to the NBA Finals in 1975–76, his third
year. In February of his 14th season (1986–87), he
was fired and replaced by Van Arsdale. Phoenix
went 14–12 the rest of the way. Its 36–46 finish
was even harder for fans because of a drug scandal
that involved six Suns players.

General manager Jerry Colangelo created the
only ownership change the team has known. In
1986–87, Colangelo formed a group of investors
and purchased the Suns from original owners
Richard Bloch, Don Diamond, and Don Pitt.

Chambers had a huge effect on the Suns after
signing with the team in 1988. During the five
years he played in Phoenix, the team increased its

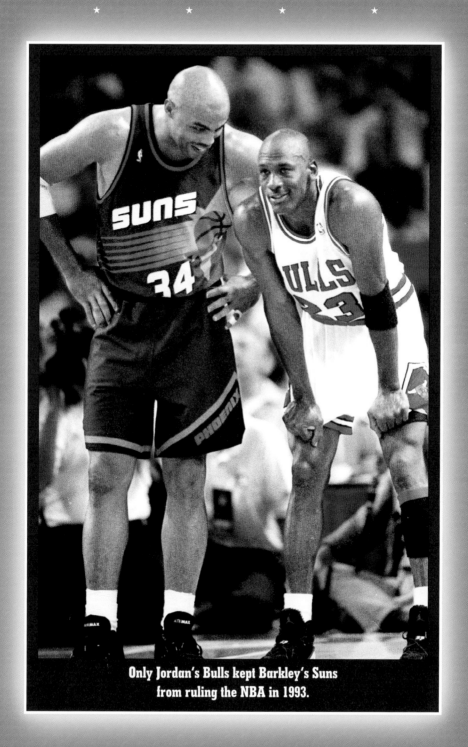

Only Jordan's Bulls kept Barkley's Suns from ruling the NBA in 1993.

Guard Stephon Marbury is one key to the Suns' future.

The Suns and Celtics played perhaps the greatest game in NBA history during the 1976 Finals. Phoenix's Garfield Heard made a memorable buzzer beater to tie Game 5 in the second overtime, but the Celtics prevailed 128-126 in three extra sessions.

victory total by 27 games in his first season, reached the Western Conference finals twice, and made it to the NBA Finals once, in 1992–93.

That was the season Paul Westphal came home to coach his old team, which now included forward Charles Barkley and **shooting guard** Danny Ainge. The two newcomers teamed up with KJ and forward Dan Majerle to lead the Suns to a 62–20 regular-season record, but Chicago's John Paxson ended their dream with a last-second 3-point shot in Game 6 of the NBA Finals.

After 13 straight playoff appearances, the Suns missed the NBA postseason in 2001–02. They returned in 2002–03, grabbing the Western Conference's eighth and last playoff spot. The team's fortunes in coming years will be pinned heavily on guard Stephon Marbury and forward Amare Stoudemire.

THE PORTLAND TRAIL BLAZERS

The Portland Trail Blazers were named in honor of the westward exploration led by Lewis and Clark. Their travels took them from the mouth of the Missouri River to the Pacific Ocean and what is now the northwest tip of Oregon in 1805.

The first basketball Trail Blazers were coached by Rolland Todd and led by forward Geoff Petrie, who later would become the team's general manager. The team began its quest in 1970–71, its first season, with a 29–53 record. Seven years later, the Blazers were NBA champions.

After struggling with four coaches in six seasons, the team hired Dr. Jack Ramsay. His first season in Portland was the third one for center Bill Walton, the NBA's No. 1 draft pick in 1974 and a two-time National Collegiate Athletic Association (NCAA) champion at University of California, Los Angeles (UCLA). The Blazers, with a supporting cast that included forward Maurice Lucas and guards Dave Twardzik and Lionel Hollins, beat the Julius Erving–led Philadelphia 76ers in the NBA Finals in six games.

Ramsay's coaching years in Portland brought more postseason appearances but no return to the title round. Late in the Ramsay era, in 1983, the team drafted Clyde "the Glide" Drexler, who would become a perennial All-Star. Drexler who played 11 $\frac{1}{2}$ years in Portland and would be a key part of the Blazers' return to the NBA Finals in 1989–90.

But not under Ramsay, who was fired in 1986 and replaced by Mike Schuler. Schuler took the club to a 49–33 record in 1986–87 and was named NBA Coach of the Year.

In 1988, owner Larry Weinberg sold the Blazers to Paul Allen, a cofounder of Microsoft. Rick

When healthy, Bill Walton was one of the NBA's best big men.

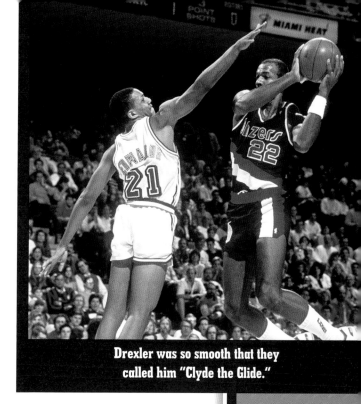

Drexler was so smooth that they called him "Clyde the Glide."

Adelman took over as head coach in 1988–89, and the Blazers, led by Drexler, **power forward** Buck Williams, and point guard Terry Porter, reached the NBA Finals before losing to Detroit.

In 1989, the Blazers added power forward Jerome Kersey. The following year, they were knocked out of the playoffs in the Western Conference finals by the Lakers, but they got back in the NBA Finals in 1991–92. After being eliminated from the playoffs in the next two years, the Blazers fired Adelman and hired P. J. Carlesimo to coach a team that now had Rod Strickland at point guard, Harvey Grant at power forward, and small forward Cliff Robinson as its scoring leader.

The Blazers traded Drexler in 1994–95, the club's last season at Portland Memorial Coliseum before moving to its jazzy new digs, the Rose Garden. In 1995–96, Arvydas Sabonis, a 31-year-old

Center Bill Walton was the most recognizable player on Portland's 1977 NBA champions. But the team's leading scorer that year was forward Maurice Lucas, who averaged 20.2 points per game.

Arvydas Sabonis was a force in the middle for the Trail Blazers.

Lithuanian rookie center who had played six years in the Spanish League, joined the team. Soon, there was another round of roster changes. Out went Strickland and Grant in a trade with Washington for power forward Rasheed Wallace. Portland's new shooting guard was Isaiah Rider and its new point guard Kenny Anderson. After yet another first-round playoff exit, its new head coach was Mike Dunleavy.

Damon Stoudamire, a Portland native, became the Blazers' point guard in Dunleavy's first year. The following year, 1998–99, Portland made it to the Western Conference finals. In 1999–2000, the Blazers picked up veteran small forward Scottie Pippen and made it to the Western Conference finals before losing to the Lakers in Game 7.

Things came unglued in 2000–01, as the Blazers went 8–14 at the end of the regular season and were eliminated by the Lakers in the first round of the playoffs. With Maurice Cheeks coaching the next two years, the Blazers made the playoffs both times, both after similar dull efforts in the latter part of the regular season. Still, Portland's trip to the playoffs in 2002–03 would be the team's 26th playoff appearance in 27 years.

CHAPTER 6

THE SACRAMENTO KINGS

Y ou'll hear cowbells clanging and voices screaming at Sacramento's Arco Arena, in hopes of a first-ever NBA championship for California's capital city. It's been more than five decades since this franchise—which has lived in five cities—won the title.

The team began life in 1948 as the Rochester Royals. The Royals were kings of the NBA in 1950–51, coached by owner–general manager Les Harrison and led on the court by guards Bob Davies and Bobby Wanzer and forward Arnie Risen.

The Royals moved to Cincinnati in 1957. They became known as the Kings when they began splitting their time between Kansas City and Omaha in 1972. Kansas City was the team's sole home in 1975, and it reached Sacramento in 1985. Sacramento remained in the Midwest Division for three years before joining the Pacific at the outset of the 1988–89 season.

Under the community-friendly ownership of

Oscar Robertson wowed NBA fans with his athletic ability.

brothers Joe and Gavin Maloof and the coaching of Rick Adelman, the Kings have been one of the NBA's most entertaining and successful teams. Their mainstay has been center Chris Webber, with support from small forward Predrag Stojokovic, veteran power forward Vlade Divac, shooting guard Doug Christie, and point guard Mike Bibby—along with reserves Bobby Jackson and Hedo Turkoglu.

Looking back, the 1963–64 team, led by then top draft pick Oscar Robertson and forward Jerry Lucas, marked a high point in the franchise's first two decades. Robertson, considered the game's best all-around player in an era that included Bill Russell and Wilt Chamberlain, was second in the NBA in scoring (with 31.4 points per game, just behind Chamberlain) and 16th in rebounding (9.9 per game). He carried the Royals to the Eastern Division playoffs, where they lost to Boston in seven games.

The Royals' last years in Cincinnati were highlighted by the arrival of center Sam Lacey and Nate "Tiny" Archibald in the 1970 draft. Archibald was second in the NBA in scoring during his second season, 1971–72, with 28.2 points per game, and in 1972–73 became the first player to lead the league in both scoring and **assists.**

The team still had a long route to Sacramento. A group of Kansas City businessmen bought the club in 1972 and sold it to a group of Sacramento businessmen in 1983. The NBA approved the move to California in 1985. Former Celtics great Bill Russell coached the team for part of the 1986–87 season before being reassigned to the team's front office. In 1995–96, the Kings made the playoffs for the second time in their new home (the first being in 1985–86). The team was coached by Garry St. Jean and led by shooting guard Mitch Richmond.

Forward Corliss Williamson came aboard in 1997–98, and new coach Rick Adelman started the

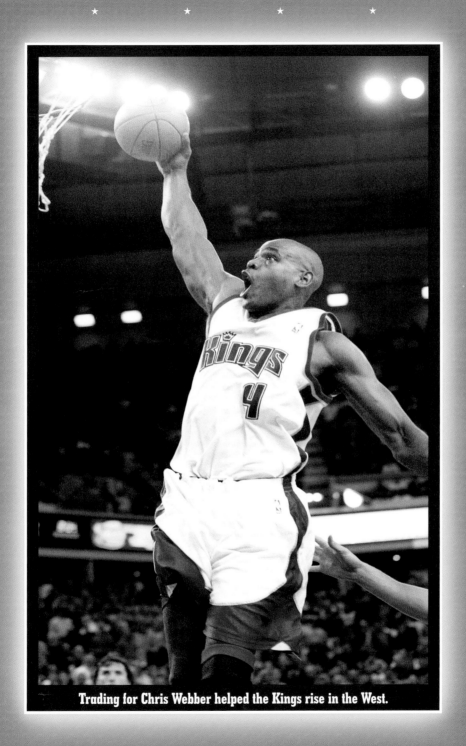

Trading for Chris Webber helped the Kings rise in the West.

Vlade Divac is the Kings' man in the middle.

next season in 1998–99. During Adelman's first season, the team added Webber (in a trade for Richmond with Washington), Divac, and point guard Jason Williams, and took Utah to Game 5 of the first round of the playoffs. It was the first sign of the Kings' new role as a force in the Pacific Division.

In 2001–02, Sacramento set a franchise record of 61 regular-season victories (the NBA's best that season). The 2002–03 team won 59 games (one shy of San Antonio's league-best 60) and made the playoffs for the fifth straight year. Since 2000–01, the team has won at least 50 games in every regular season. Before that, only Rochester in 1949–50 (51 games) and Cincinnati in 1963–64 (55) had won so many games. It's a new day for a franchise that, since its inaugural season in 1948–49, has won at least half its regular-season games only 19 times.